STEM Milestones
Historic Inventions and Discoveries

THE
TEMPERATURE SCALES
OF FAHRENHEIT
AND CELSIUS

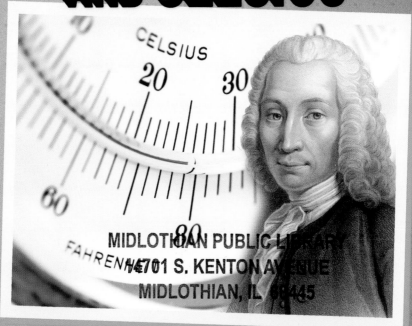

Eileen S. Coates

PowerKiDS
press.

New York

Published in 2019 by The Rosen Publishing Group, Inc.
29 East 21st Street, New York, NY 10010

First Edition

Editor: Tanya Dellaccio
Book Design: Reann Nye

Photo Credits: Cover (Anders Celsius), p. 1 Chronicle/Alamy Stock Photo; cover (thermometer), p. 1 seewhatmitchsee/Shutterstock.com; pp. 5 (Anders Celsius), 8, 11 Science & Society Picture Library/SSPL/Getty Images; p. 5 (thermometer) Tomas Ragina/Shutterstock.com; p. 7 Culture Club/Hulton Archive/Getty Images; p. 9 Paul McKinnon/Shutterstock.com; p. 13 Bettmann/Getty Images; p. 14 https://commons.wikimedia.org/wiki/File:Headshot_of_Anders_Celsius.jpg; p. 15 Boyer/Roger Viollet/Getty Images; p. 17 MU YEE TING/Shutterstock.com; p. 18 Zmaj88/Shutterstock.com; p. 19 thaisign/Shutterstock.com; p. 20 https://commons.wikimedia.org/wiki/File:Lord_Kelvin_photograph.jpg.

Cataloging-in-Publication Data

Names: Coates, Eileen S.
Title: The temperature scales of fahrenheit and celsius / Eileen S. Coates.
Description: New York : PowerKids Press, 2019. | Series: STEM milestones: historic inventions and discoveries | Includes glossary and index.
Identifiers: ISBN 9781538345245 (pbk.) | ISBN 9781538343593 (library bound) | ISBN 9781538345252 (6 pack)
Subjects: LCSH: Fahrenheit, Daniel Gabriel, 1686-1736–Juvenile literature. | Celsius, Anders, 1701-1744–Juvenile literature. | Physicists–Poland–Biography–Juvenile literature. | Temperature measurements–Juvenile literature. | Thermometers–Juvenile literature.

Classification: LCC QC15.C59 2019 | DDC 536'.50287 B–dc23

Manufactured in the United States of America

CPSIA Compliance Information: Batch #CWPK19. For Further Information contact Rosen Publishing, New York, New York at 1-800-237-9932

CONTENTS

TELLING TEMPERATURES

Temperature is a measurement that we use in our everyday lives. It tells us how hot or cold something—such as the weather or our body—is. There wasn't always a good way to measure those things, though. Daniel Gabriel Fahrenheit and Anders Celsius were two scientists who lived hundreds of years ago. They made measuring and reading temperatures a lot easier for everyone.

Fahrenheit created a thermometer. Thermometers are the instruments that we use to measure temperatures. Fahrenheit and Celsius each created a scale of numbers that helped people read the thermometer. We use their inventions and discoveries every day!

You've probably heard the name "Fahrenheit" before. People often say the name of his scale when reading a temperature.

ANDERS CELSIUS

°C °F

50 120
40 100
30 80
20 60
10
0 40
10 20
20 0
30 20

CELSIUS AND FAHRENHEIT
THERMOMETER

5

A MAN OF SCIENCE

Daniel Gabriel Fahrenheit was born on May 24, 1686, in Gdańsk, Poland. His parents, Daniel and Concordia, died when he was 15 years old.

After his parents' death, Fahrenheit moved to Amsterdam, in the Netherlands. He started making scientific instruments, which are the tools scientists use to do experiments. This helped him learn a lot about the different **substances** used to make them. During this time, he learned about the first thermometers, which were being made in Italy.

Fahrenheit traveled to many different cities to learn new things about his craft before he settled in The Hague, in the Netherlands.

PALACE AT THE HAGUE

7

FAHRENHEIT'S THERMOMETER

While in The Hague, Fahrenheit became a glassblower, a person who makes things out of glass by blowing air into very hot glass. One of the things he made when he was a glassblower was a new type of thermometer.

GLASS TUBE

BULB

FASCINATING FINDINGS

Fahrenheit's thermometers each had a little bulb at the bottom that held the alcohol. As the temperature increased, the alcohol would rise up a thin glass tube. The tube was equally wide from top to bottom, which helped the alcohol rise at a steady rate.

His first thermometers, which he invented in 1709, were glass tubes with **alcohol** at the bottom. The alcohol took up more space in the tube as it got warmer. Since the thermometers weren't all the same, it was hard to get an **accurate** reading. Fahrenheit decided to create thermometers and measurements that would be **universal**. This means that when someone read the temperature on the thermometer, everyone would understand what it meant.

MAKING A SCALE

As he got better at making the thermometers, Fahrenheit began creating his temperature scale. He did this by setting numbers to certain things. He mixed salt, ice, and water, and measured its coldest temperature, which he decided would be 0 **degrees** on his scale. He decided the temperature of the human body was 96 degrees, which would be the top of the scale. This scale later changed.

Later, Fahrenheit figured out how to use liquid mercury instead of alcohol in his thermometers. Mercury is a silver metal that's liquid at room temperature. Since mercury rises at a slower and steadier rate than alcohol, it made the thermometer easier to read. He **introduced** his scale to the public in 1724.

FASCINATING FINDINGS

Fahrenheit discovered a way to clean the mercury so that it didn't stick to the glass in the thermometer. This is what makes it possible for the mercury to rise up the tube to measure the temperature.

In 1714, Fahrenheit created the mercury thermometer. Today, there isn't mercury in most thermometers because it can be very harmful to people.

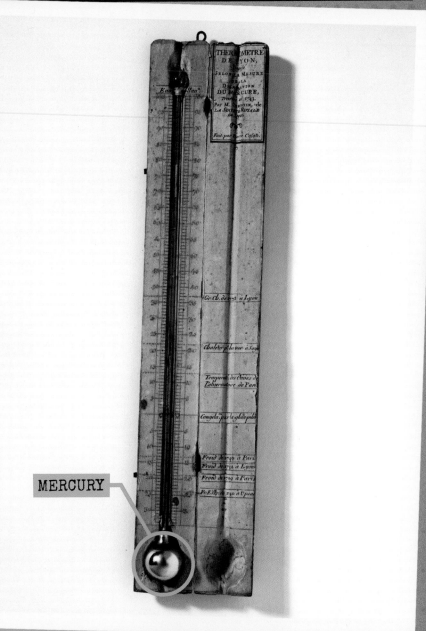

MERCURY

GETTING IT RIGHT

Fahrenheit's scale changed a bit over time. As more **precise** ways to measure things were found, he got better temperature readings. The freezing point of water is now known to be 32 degrees on Fahrenheit's scale, and the boiling point of water is 212 degrees. The human body temperature was found to be 98.6 degrees, instead of Fahrenheit's original 96 degrees.

In 1736, Fahrenheit died in The Hague, the Netherlands. The Fahrenheit scale is still the main scale used to measure temperature in the United States.

Fahrenheit changed his scale so that there were 180 degrees between the freezing point and boiling point of water.

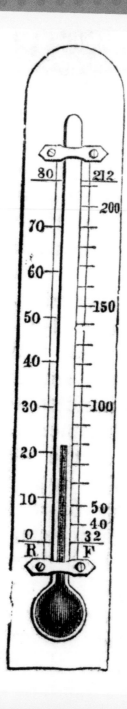

13

A FAMILY OF SCIENTISTS

Anders Celsius—the inventor of the Celsius temperature scale—was born in Uppsala, Sweden, on November 17, 1701. He came from a family of scientists. His father was an **astronomy** teacher at a college. One of Anders's grandfathers studied astronomy, too!

ANDERS CELSIUS

Anders went to Uppsala University and, like his father and grandfather, began teaching astronomy there in 1730. While teaching, he began studying the aurora borealis, which are bright lights in the sky that can be seen in the far north. They're also known as the northern lights.

THE NORTHERN LIGHTS

Celsius continued to study the aurora borealis and discovered that it's related to Earth's magnetic field. Earth acts like a huge magnet, and Earth's magnetic field is the area where the magnetism can be felt. The field makes tiny **particles** from the sun move toward the most magnetic places on Earth, which are called magnetic poles. The particles crash into particles in the **atmosphere**, which is what causes the lights.

Earth's magnetic field is what makes **compasses** point north. A compass helps people figure out what direction they're facing, which in turn helps them figure out which direction they need to go to reach somewhere.

FASCINATING FINDINGS

Celsius also traveled with a group of scientists to measure the length between one meridian and the next. Meridians are imaginary lines that connect Earth's northernmost and southernmost points. Scientists break Earth into 360 evenly spaced meridians. Their measurements gave clues to Earth's shape.

Celsius's studies on Earth and its magnetic fields helped him make other discoveries, too. He used his findings to draw other conclusions about temperature and how it works.

NORTHERN LIGHTS

THE CELSIUS SCALE

Along with studying Earth's magnetic field, Celsius began studying temperature scales and ways in which they could be easier to understand. He came up with a scale that was simpler and easier to use than Fahrenheit's. It's known as the Celsius scale.

FASCINATING FINDINGS

Celsius discovered that the reason the boiling point of water isn't the same everywhere is because of a place's atmospheric pressure. This is how hard the air in a certain place presses down on Earth. The lower the atmospheric pressure is, the lower the boiling point of water is.

Celsius set the freezing point of water at
0 degrees and set the boiling point of water
at 100 degrees. He did many experiments
on the freezing and boiling points of water
to test his scale. He found that the freezing
point of water is the same everywhere on
Earth, but the boiling point of water is not.

SCIENTIFIC SCALES

Thermometers today are a lot more advanced than Fahrenheit's original invention, but they're made possible because of his milestones in science. Fahrenheit and Celsius's temperature scales gave us a way to figure out how hot or cold something was in a way that could be understood by everyone. Even though the two scales are different, people can do math to change one measurement to another.

WILLIAM THOMPSON

FASCINATING FINDINGS

Modern scientists also use the Kelvin scale. William Thompson, who was also called Lord Kelvin, came up with this temperature scale. On it, 0 degrees is the coldest temperature possible.

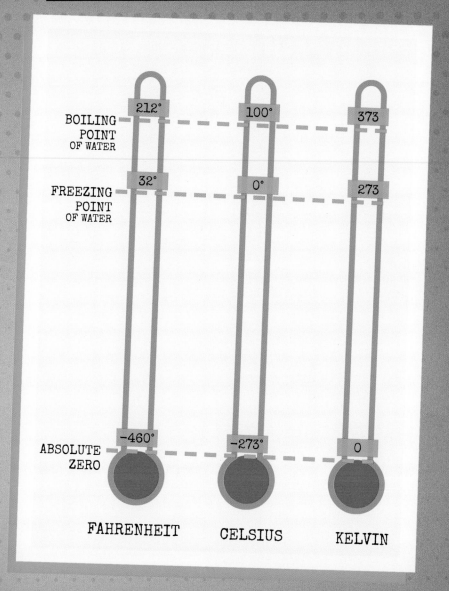

Both Fahrenheit and Celsius contributed a lot to science. Their inventions and discoveries make it possible for us to measure temperature!

THE LIVES OF DANIEL GABRIEL FAHRENHEIT AND ANDERS CELSIUS

May 24, 1686
Daniel Gabriel
Fahrenheit is born in
Gdańsk, Poland.

November 27, 1701
Anders Celsius is born
in Uppsala, Sweden.

1709
Fahrenheit invents
the first alcohol
thermometer

1714
Fahrenheit invents his
mercury thermometer.

1724
Fahrenheit introduces
his temperature scale
to the world.

1736
Celsius travels to
Lapland to measure
Earth's meridians.

September 16, 1736
Fahrenheit dies in
The Hague.

1742
Celsius introduces his
temperature scale.

April 25, 1744
Celsius dies in
Uppsala, Sweden.

GLOSSARY

accurate: Free of mistakes.

alcohol: A clear liquid sometimes used in medicines and other products.

astronomy: The study of stars, planets, and other heavenly bodies.

atmosphere: The whole mass of air that surrounds Earth.

compass: A tool that shows direction.

degree: A unit, or certain amount, used for measuring temperature.

introduce: To cause something to begin to be used.

particle: A very small piece of matter.

precise: Very exact.

substance: A matter of a certain kind.

universal: True at all times or places.

INDEX

WEBSITES

Due to the changing nature of Internet links, PowerKids Press has
developed an online list of websites related to the subject of this
book. This site is updated regularly. Please use this link to access
the list: www.powerkidslinks.com/hiad/temp